# 21 Business and Marketing
# LESSONS FROM A
# PROSTITUTE

I0393493

Seductive
Street
Secrets
From The
World's
Oldest
Profession
To
Improve
Your
Results
In Any
Business

Leon Jay

For further information and support please contact:

support@fusionhq.com
www.LessonsFromAProstitute.com

"I honestly believe that advertising is the most fun you can have with your clothes on"

Jerry Della Femina

# CONTENTS

Forward (rewind) ...................................................... 1

Driven to Sex ............................................................. 7

More Than Just Boobs .......................................... 15

Are You Willing? .................................................... 21

Do You Need A Prostitute? ................................... 25

The Chase Is On ..................................................... 31

Good Girls Get Paid More ..................................... 37

Even Frankenstein Can Get Laid .......................... 41

Getting Into The Right Position ............................ 47

Controlling Your Man ............................................. 51

Helping The Enemy ................................................ 57

Beyond Sex ............................................................. 63

Not All Men Were Created Equal .......................... 69

2 Girls Are Better Than 1 ...................................... 75

The Honest Criminal .............................................. 79

F..K You .................................................................. 83

Who Is In Control? ................................................. 87

Buying Boobs ........................................................... 93

Don't Be Too Mature ............................................. 97

Prostitutes That Suck ............................................ 101

She Did What? ...................................................... 105

Pimping ................................................................ 111

Climax .................................................................. 115

# FORWARD (REWIND)

*"What we see depends mainly
on what we look for"*

John Lubbock

This book perhaps needs a little explanation.

The idea came while speaking at a marketing event in the world's capital of prostitution – Pattaya, Thailand.

Pattaya, if you are not familiar with it, is a tourist coastal city not far from Bangkok. It is made up of street after street of bars, Go-Go clubs, erotic shows, dubious massage shops and girls wearing very little.

I have been asked to speak there several times now and each time I go I am in business mode, so perhaps see it a little differently than most tourists who visit.

When you live and breathe business and marketing you tend to see it all around you. And so it was with these eyes that I took a look at the world's oldest profession and asked the question "how do these girls make a living in such a competitive environment?"

What I saw astounded me. Almost none of the girls here have any business or marketing experience, or formal training (no surprise there). Yet they practised many advanced business strategies better than the majority of business owners that I know.

I began to take notes. Here was a learning opportunity unlike any other. Here was an industry that understood the concept that 'sex sells' better than any other.

What I want to share with you in this book are a range of insights gained and demonstrated by what is arguably one of the most intriguing and controversial industries on the planet.

Many of you will know that I have spent many years living in Thailand. During this time I have studied Thai culture and grown a fondness and appreciation for the Thai people and the Thai way of life. However I have to say that Pattaya is very unlike the rest of Thailand (with the exception of small parts of Bangkok and Phuket). It is unique in almost every way.

I would like to clarify for anyone not having visited Thailand that you should not judge Thailand based on the content of this book. In fact I would recommend putting any judgements aside and simply learn from the examples given so well by these girls who must compete every night against thousands of others to make a living.

One wise man once said we are all prostitutes for the right price. Perhaps you are already prostituting yourself every day in a job you hate. Selling your body and mind to a boss you hate for an hourly rate much less than that of any self-respecting prostitute.

Once during my travels around Australia I met a local girl who was an ex-call girl. She explained that she had only stopped her trade because of her children. She actually had enjoyed the work and considered herself as providing a service that brought pleasure to people's lives.

She was careful about the clients she accepted and never did anything that she was not willing or wanted to do. In this regard I realized actually she had more self-respect than many employees of traditional jobs.

Life is on average only 4000 weeks long. How many of these weeks have you already sold for someone else's benefit? If you currently have a job you hate how many more weeks are you willing to sell to it?

If there is one thing I have learned, it is that life is rarely black and white.

Many of those we may consider to be below us socially have so much to teach us if only we get our egos, judgments and arrogance out of the way.

We have a lot to learn, so let the journey begin…

# DRIVEN TO SEX

*"Motivation is a battle for the heart,
not just an appeal to the mind"*

Patrick Dixon

The reason most of us do anything in business is the hope of making money. And in this regard on a superficial level the prostitutes of Pattaya (commonly called bar girls due to the fact they usually hang out in bars to look for customers) are no different.

However in most cases their motivation to do what they do is far beyond themselves. In other words they don't do it just for personal financial gain.

Personally I always had the image of prostitutes plying their trade to fund a drug habit, or perhaps a high class escort funding a lavish lifestyle. Although this may be the reason for some, in most cases I found it was to support their family.

Most come from very poor backgrounds and are trying to support their sick parents, a child (many are single mums whose family look after the child while the girl sends money back), or in some cases they are funding a university education so they can build a better life for themselves and their family.

Not surprisingly most have no desire to do what they do. However unlike many western countries there is no social security and very limited job opportunities. Severe circumstance creates the motivation to move to Pattaya and literally sell themselves to meet these family obligations.

Indeed looking after the family financially is a social expectation throughout Thai culture, no matter what the choice of profession. It is the children who look after their parents, grandparents, and brothers or sisters who may also need their help.

So engrained is this sense of responsibility it can drive many girls to these extreme measures.

These girls don't grow up thinking 'I want to be a bar girl'. Most come from the countryside, not the cities. In the country especially, attitudes towards sex are still very conservative with many girls having to marry the first man they sleep with.

The lifestyle of Pattaya is worlds removed and so it takes a huge mental and emotional shift to allow them to go from country girl to Pattaya bar girl. And it is the motivation of supporting their family that allows them to do this.

OK, so what does this have to do with you and your business?

Basically with a big enough reason you will be amazed of what you are capable.

Despite the claims of many gurus, to get a successful business up and running usually requires some degree of sacrifice. This may be financial, time and/or effort on tasks you would rather not have to do. Usually a combination of all three.

If you lack motivation the chances are you will fail.

At some time during the growth of your business you will face challenges and setbacks. You will have to do things you don't want to do. And the chances are you will require some huge mental and emotional shifts to get yourself to take the financial risks, invest the time or force yourself to take the action necessary to succeed.

Just like the bar girls from Pattaya it will be your motivation that enables and drives these shifts to take place.

I can't give you motivation – that is something that must come from within. All I can do is suggest where to look for it. And no, it is not in some overpriced rah-rah seminar.

For different people different motivators will work better than others.

Perhaps for you it is in avoiding pain. This usually comes in the form of financial pain. Maybe you can't pay the bills, you have a loved one that needs your assistance or you are simply frustrated at never having enough.

Another form of pain maybe the feeling of being stuck in a 9-5 job you hate. Maybe it is the idea of siting in rush hour traffic just one more day, or having to face another day of being unappreciated and undervalued at work.

Or your motivation may come in the form of desire.

Desire to buy a new house, a new car or even a private airplane. Desire to build a company of your own or to make an idea a reality. Desire to create flexibility in your lifestyle, to work when you want, where you want.

For me motivation comes from the desire to create. To create new ideas, projects and businesses. I believe we are at some level all creative and the creative force is one of the most powerful of all.

As I said, I can't tell you what your personal motivation or motivations are. The one thing I would suggest is you look to something bigger than personal gain.

Not that there is anything wrong in wanting more, or having a new house or car on your goals list. Just that if this is your only motivation then your success will be short lived and you will always be left wanting more. You will never truly feel fulfilled.

Psychology studies have shown we are more likely to act in the avoidance of pain than in the pursuit of pleasure.

In reality it is unlikely you will have one single motivator. Instead your motivation will be made of multiple reasons; pain, desire and creativity.

The important thing is that you are clear on your motivations. Remind yourself of them regularly as they will kick start you into action and then carry you through challenging or difficult periods and tasks.

True of normal jobs as well as for entrepreneurs or prostitutes, focusing only on money will almost certainly lead to problems.

In the case of the girls from Pattaya many turn to alcohol and drugs to help them cope with their new life style. Those who don't learn to focus on their original reason for moving there soon become depressed and angry.

Years ago when I practiced as a therapist I would see the same pattern in the 9-5 prostitutes (those working jobs they hated just to pay the bills). They would turn to alcohol or drugs as a form of distraction, or to mask the depression that this way of life can cause.

Anger at themselves for living this way can often lead to blaming others, society or 'the system'.

Change is the only solution.

Either change your situation or change your perception.

By creating purpose in your life you are better able to accept the pain in getting to where you want to go.

I recently saw an interview with an Olympic athlete that was asked if he enjoyed the training. He said that much of the time it was painful hard work, but he did it anyway because he knew it was what was required to get gold. And he really wanted gold.

Never lose sight of the goal. If you focus only on the money it is only a matter of time before the negative feelings set in.

Make a vision board in your office, or better still use some software such as www.MyDesktopTherapist.com (it's free) to keep you focused on your goals, motivations and purpose.

# MORE THAN JUST BOOBS

*"The customer experience is the
next competitive battleground"*

Jerry Gregoire, CIO, Dell Computer

No market place is as crowded as the bars of Pattaya. You have to see it to believe it.

Street after street of girls hanging out of bars, dancing semi naked on tables, totally naked in go-go bar after go-go bar, working in massage shops or simply walking the streets trying to seduce a customer.

Yes, there are a lot of punters there. But there are far, far more girls than potential customers.

It may be easy to think that is it just a case of the best looking girls win, but it is far from that simple.

Sure, the really hot girls have no problem. Their exceptional looks alone are enough to secure interest. However these girls are rare. Most are far more average looking and must work a lot harder to compete.

First they must get the attention of a prospect. In most places if a girls dresses in a suggestive way she will get some attention. In Pattaya where most of the girls are dressed to impress this is far from enough.

Indeed when you are surrounded by literally thousands of girls who are all scantily dressed it is essential to find another way to stand out.

Many learn to shout at prospects, usually something along the lines of 'hey handsome man – come here'. This certainly works for some of the new arrivals in town, but it is soon tuned out by most prospects who have been there for more than a few days (or hours).

Instead to be successful they must put their full focus on one customer at a time. They must catch their eye, communicate directly with them and build rapport.

It is amazing how quickly the girls there learn to speak English. It is almost essential for their economic survival. Many even learn to speak some Japanese, Korean, German and Russian (some of the most common customer nationalities there). By communicating in a language that your customer understands you increase your chances of building rapport, and ultimately making a sale.

How does this apply to your business?

It is important to get the attention of your prospect, we all know that. The trick is learning how to look them directly in the eye and let them know we have something of interest or benefit for them.

The first step to achieving this may seem obvious, but so few businesses do it well. This first step is to be stood in front of a genuine prospect to start with.

The bar girls do this by being in bars or areas they know that a lot of men (and some women) are actively looking for sex. Not everyone here is a potential customer. Pattaya is also a popular tourist destination for Thai's, some are there just out of curiosity and others (like myself) go there on business. However many are there just for the sex.

You need to ask yourself 'how can I get in front of my potential customer base?', and 'how can I get their attention?'

The next step is to make eye contact. In business this is essentially engaging the prospect's interest, letting them know you have more for them than what firsts meets the eye. We want to connect 1-1 with them.

For many businesses, especially those online, literally connecting 1-1 is not possible. However we can form our communications to talk to the prospect as an individual, as though we were talking to them 1-1.

Engage the customer with your marketing materials in a way that lets them know that you do understand their needs and their desires, and that you can satisfy them both.

One of the tricks that copywriters use to help them with this is to build a customer profile.

This is essentially a description of an individual from their target market. This would include their age, gender, financial income, education, religion, where they lived, what their hobbies are, what their pains and regrets are, what their hopes and dreams are and even their name.

When you have a vivid image of this person in your mind then talk to them directly in your videos, sales letters, web pages, brochures or advertising. It is also important to understand and use the language of your customer. As with the bar girls, speaking the same language is not essential, but it does increase conversion rates.

In the case of business if your audience is English then you will of course communicate in English. However look at ways to communicate using the language patterns and niche terminology of your prospects.

For example if your typical customer is highly educated and you are selling golfing products you would want to match your vocabulary and grammar to suit this audience.

If you are selling weight loss products your demographic is likely to consist of a much wider audience. In this case you need to make sure your language is understood by all education levels.

The bar girl knows that if she can engage a customer in conversation she will increase her chances of making a sale. Your job is no different. Place yourself in front of a perspective audience, capture attention and engage in conversation.

# ARE YOU WILLING?

*"What we obtain too cheaply, we esteem too lightly; it's dearness only that gives everything its value"*

Thomas Payne

In Pattaya there are plenty of girls working the bars from 9-5, but they also know this is not when they are going to get the most business.

If a girl is to make a good living she obviously needs to be prepared to work at night too. Bottom line is if you are going to be a successful prostitute you need to take action outside of 9-5.

Hardly a revelation in the sex industry, but it is just as true for almost any other business too.

I do not know a single successful entrepreneur or business owner that has not put in long hours outside of 9-5. And I know a lot.

All have put in late nights, early mornings and long weekends.

For some this may be due to the nature of the business. For example in my case running promotions in different time zones or communicating with team members around the world. For others (again myself included) it may be the need to meet deadlines. For almost all of us it is also the passion of what we do that makes the clock irrelevant.

As an employee you are conditioned to watch the clock. Most are just waiting for it to reach 5pm so they can go home and do something else.

If you ever find yourself watching the clock for knock off time when you are building your business chances are you are in the wrong business. This is not to say you must work 16 hours a day, 7 days a week all the time. Just that you must be more flexible with your ideas around working times.

Personally I have little concept of what day of the week it is. Sunday is just as good a day to work as Wednesday. (Actually I prefer Sunday to work and Wednesday to rest as during the week shops are open and scenic places less crowded.)

My working day usually begins at 4-6am. And no, I don't have an alarm clock. I can usually focus at this time in the morning better than any other as there are few distractions. This allows me to get more done by the time most people are just getting warmed up at work than many will achieve all day.

It is still important to take time off to relax and enjoy life. Some weeks I will work very, very hard. Others very little. Some days it makes more sense to work later due to the nature of international business, other days very early.

The trick is to simply let go of this 9-5 mentality and focus more on what times and durations makes sense for you and your business. If you are in 'the zone' then take advantage of it. If you are in need of a break then listen to your body and take a rest – regardless of the time or what day it is.

# DO YOU NEED A PROSTITUTE?

*"What you need and what you want aren't the same things"*

Cherise Sinclair

I have heard it said many times that to be successful you find a need and you fill it. Or that you should focus on people's needs as this type of product will always be bought even in times of economic depression.

Makes logical sense. But is it true?

It could be argued whether sex is a need or a desire. Certainly in regards to sex tourism though it is based more in desire than need.

Prostitution is considered the oldest profession in the world. Indeed it was actually a brothel that created the world's first bank. Even the first coins of the Roman Empire were created to exchange for sexual services.

Therefore the sex industry has survived every economic recession, and remains almost unchanged in centuries. (The coins that the Romans used depicted the type of sexual act that was to be performed in exchange for the coin, and the relative value of those sexual acts remains the same today.)

In the case of Pattaya the girls are certainly focused on the desires of the prospects. And not just in a purely sexual way...

I saw a documentary on prostitution once where the women interviewed claimed that many of their clients did not even want sex. They just wanted company and to feel like someone cared for them.

Many of the bar girls appear to have figured this out too. While they may be exposing a lot of flesh, they are also stroking the ego of each prospect.

By focusing their attention on one individual, telling them how handsome they are (even if everyone knows this is not true) and by touching the customers in a caring (not just sexual) way, they connect with a desire far deeper than sex. That is the desire to be appreciated by another.

In main stream business we too need to focus on customer's desires, and caring for the customer.

Even during a recession many of us need to buy a new computer or new cell phone. Yet do we need to buy an Apple product?

Of course not, yet Apple were one of the few companies to continue to grow during an economic downturn. Despite that for most of us we could function just as well with a cheap PC, Android phone (if indeed you 'need' a smart phone at all) or generic MP3 player.

There are of course many luxury brands that suffered, so it is not so simple to say that luxury products do well, but neither can you say that need beats desire.

The problem with needs based products is that usually people's needs are already being met. Few of us need for much these days. And once we have our needs met changing brands or supplier often requires some type of incentive or motivation to make that change.

Basically we are creatures of habit. Therefore we are unlikely to try a new type of soap for example, just because it is on the shelf.

As a business owner, marketer or copywriter our job is to build desire in the customer regardless of the product or service we are selling. As a start-up business or product developer we need to ensure that there is the potential in our product to create this desire.

Digital information products that do well are typically those that help solve a problem (help you lose weight, find a mate, overcome an illness, make more money etc). These work well because large numbers of people already have the desire to change. As long as you can build belief that your information will help them do that then you have a sale.

Other products may require more social positioning, or appeal to the desire of improving the owners lifestyle image (think Apple). These will usually require great design, branding and marketing to connect this desire to your product.

However, even if your product or service is something more practical, for example a plumber, you can still focus on desire in your marketing.

People want to trust the person they are hiring. People want to know a quality job will be done. People want to know it will be done quickly and that the plumber will be on time. Just replace the word want for desire and you can see what I mean.

Whatever your business, create and focus on desires and you will increase your success.

On a side note there is often a misconception about the Asian sex trade. Many westerners believe that the most customers are tourists. Actually Thai men make up the majority of the customers for the sex trade in

Thailand (though not in central Pattaya which is aimed for foreign business).

Even in a poor country there are still plenty of people willing to pay. So long as the desire is strong enough people will find a way. This is why there is so much credit card debt in the West for electronics that people want, but can't afford.

# THE CHASE IS ON

*"Persistence wears down resistance"*

William J Federer

You don't need to stay in Pattaya long before you start seeing plenty of Westerners having a broken English conversation with some girl who just called them. Nor will it take long before you start hearing the stories of some girl who emailed them asking for financial help for her family.

Even if you are not interested in 'going home' with a girl she will often still try and extract a phone number or email address from you.

These girls are experts at collecting contact details and following up. Better than almost every offline business and even better than many online businesses.

They have learned that 'no sale' on the first day does not mean all is lost.

A small investment for phone calls, text messages or email can often result in money later on. They can be so persistent I have known some people to block their numbers or auto delete their emails.

The truth is that once you have invested time and energy in getting the initial interest of a prospect much of the hard work has been done. By collecting contact details and then following up you can often save the sale, or make additional ones.

It goes to show no matter what business you are in you should be building a list, and following up. If the girls of Pattaya can do it so can you. No excuses.

You should take every opportunity you can to capture the name, email, phone number and/or address of both customers and prospects. Ensure they are tagged so you know when, where and why that lead was captured so you can target your follow up accordingly.

For online businesses this is easy. You simple need an offer and an optin form on your website. (For more information on this read my other book 'Do Less Work, Make More Money'.) Offline businesses may need to be more creative.

One small market owner I knew asked me how he could do this in his business. I suggested running a simple competition where people could enter to win some of his product. By doing this he had several hundred leads in just a few days.

If you have any business cards or brochures include an offer for a free gift, discount or consultation. To collect it the prospect must go to your website and fill in a form.

If you run a shop, café or service based businesses ask customers for their details to keep them updated on special offers, flash promotions or member's discounts. Supermarkets do this well by having you fill in your details for a loyalty card.

Once you have the details the next step is to follow up. Ensure you provide great content or value first.

Most bar girls will know not to ask for money immediately, but to keep working the ego first.

Messages such as 'I miss you' and 'when can I see you next?' will feed the desire to be wanted. Then they can follow up with a more direct call to action such as 'can we meet tonight?' or 'my mother is sick, can you send me some money to help'. (For any of you sceptics out there – yes, it does work. Not every time, but often enough to make it worthwhile trying.)

In your business look at ways you can provide value.

Deliver industry news, interesting facts, useful information and free content or samples. Incentivise people with limited time discounts or limited quantity special opportunities.

The important lesson from the bar girls is to ensure your customer does not forget you. And to let them know you have not forgotten them.

# GOOD GIRLS GET PAID MORE

*"One of the deep secrets of life is that all that is really worth doing is what we do for others"*

Lewis Carol

If a girl focuses on just the money, then a customer is likely to feel used, and only wanted for his money. While this may be technically true in most cases it misses the point of the service being offered. And again I am referring not just to the sex, but also to making him (or her) feel special.

No customer in any industry want to feel like they are being taken advantage of financially. Of course as customers we all know that a business wants our money at the end of the day. But we want to feel special are appreciated before we hand over the cash.

A successful prostitute knows this too. They will work their customers emotions and ego long before the topic of money is raised. Both parties know this will be inevitable, but the courtship is often an important part of the process.

Sure, some customers see what they want, offer the money straight up and job done. But these are the minority. If you want to access the majority then you need to understand and work with human emotions a little better.

By taking a potential client and focusing all her attention on him a girl can make him feel truly special. Even when he is not. Indeed the less attractive the customer the more likely this attention will work as he is unlikely to be used to it.

The better the focus on the customer, the better the chance for a sale. Not only that, but the better the chances for a fat tip too.

As a business owner you need to do the same.

You need to stroke your customer's errr, ego. To make them feel unique and special.

This is something that Apple did well with their stores. They have staff that are trained to look after and give assistance to each customer.

See what you can do to go the extra mile to make people feel valued and appreciated even before the first sale. Then follow up to make sure they continue to know that you care.

This will not only increase the chances of a prospect choosing you over a competitor, but also of them buying from you again, and of referring their friends. And the best leads are free, targeted leads that come with a personal recommendation from a friend.

If you put your efforts into looking after your customers, and treat prospects with the same courtesy, they will look after you

# EVEN FRANKENSTEIN CAN GET LAID

*"Don't underestimate your worth by comparing yourself with others"*

Jaachynma N.E. Agu

This lesson struck me after I was invited to see one of the famous erotic shows in Pattaya. No, not the sleazy ping pong shows, or the lady boy shows, but a proper choreographed erotic dance performance.

The show was indeed quite impressive, and the quality of the dance outstanding (these were true dance professionals). However during the intervals a group of girls would come on stage and do some simple go-go dancing in the hope of getting a customer to take them home for the night.

Most of these girls were fairly average in looks. One however was outstanding. A solid 9 in my opinion. She was like something from an advert in an exotic holiday magazine. Long perfect hair, a flawless well-proportioned body, sparkling eyes and a captivating smile.

Had I been looking for that type of service she was by far the obvious choice. Or so I thought.

Next to her, not to be too politically correct, was Frankenstein.

Perhaps one of the most scary girls I had seen in Pattaya (and that is quite an achievement). Her fake breasts were sticking out in a distorted unnatural way, her nose looked like Michael Jackson's, her face pulled back like a badly aging Hollywood movie star and makeup that looked like it belonged in a horror movie.

As a looked at this beauty and beast on the stage dancing next to each other, offering the same services and the same price I wondered how an earth Frankenstein ever made a living.

It was just at that moment some drunk (am sure he must have been) Westerner came up and pointed to the freakish looking girl on the stage and asked to take her home. At that moment I realized there truly is someone for everyone. Just some markets are more limited than others.

Here is the thing though. You don't need to, nor should you, appeal to everyone. This is one of the biggest mistakes I see many product owners make.

Look at where your strong points are and focus on people who will appreciate them. This is the principle of micro-niches. The scary looking bar girl did not need every customer who walked in to watch the show. Truth is she could probably make a decent enough living off less than 0.1% of the people who went there.

If you are selling a weight loss product by focusing on all overweight people you will find yourself with a lot of competition. Instead look at a demographic that you can hyper target. For example Asian teenage girls living in the US.

This may feel like you are alienating much of your potential audience, and to some degree you are. After all most weight loss programs are fairly universal. However by using this level of focus you can really concentrate your marketing efforts to become far more effective.

For example lets say your product is called 'Weight Loss For Asian-American Teen Girls' (hopefully you could come up with a better title, but you get the point). If an Asian teen girl saw the product she is more likely to buy it over the competition as it feels like it is targeted to her.

There is a fine line balance between micro-niching and having almost no customer base. The size of the niche will define the ability to sub-niche. So in the case of sex and weight loss the potential markets are huge. There are so many people that there is still plenty of money even in very well defined niches.

You need to make sure that your potential customer base is large enough for your business goals. This is really just a balance of common sense and some basic keyword research. (Again read a copy of my book 'Do Less Work, Make More Money' for more information on this. You can download for free at www.free.DoLessWorkMakeMoreMoney.com)

Don't be afraid to be different from your competition, or to do things differently. Indeed you should embrace your differences and highlight them. Being different will help you stand out, and to attract the attention of those who will appreciate why you are different.

# GETTING INTO THE RIGHT POSITION

*"The customer's perception is your reality"*

Kate Zabriskie

Quality perception, positioning and packaging are critical when setting a price point. Needless to say I saw this being demonstrated to the extreme in the streets of Pattaya.

I have talked about bar girls as prostitutes. In fact really they are just one type of prostitute.

In addition you also get Go-Go dancers, show girls, low class and high class escorts as well as 'massage' girls. Then you get your more stereo typical street hooker. In each case the end service may well be the same, but the bill will be different.

Why the difference?

Well apart from natural looks (which of course plays a large part in the final price they can demand) it is how they have positioned themselves (ie bar girl, show girl, escort etc). Also it is how much attention to detail they have made in the packaging (quality/style of clothing, makeup and hair etc).

Of course if they work in a top end bar, as a customer your perception is already set to expect a higher price point. In the same way where and how you position your business can affect people's perception and expectation of your business and your prices.

Again, take Apple as a superb example.

Despite many people's beliefs, Apple have actually invented very little themselves. They did not invent the desktop OS, nor the mouse, notebook, tablet, smart phone, touch screen, MP3 player, digital music store or anything else they get so much credit for.

All of these had been developed by someone else first.

What Apple did so well was to repackage and reposition each of them. They focused on design and simplicity. They appealed to those who consider themselves to be independent creative types (which actually is most of us – despite the reality).

They did not launch the 'Apple MP3 Player', they released the iPod. They did not release an 'Apple tablet', they launched the iPad. In every case Apple puts its attention in the detail of design and adds a premium price point to match.

The hardware and software may be beautiful, but the actual quality (aside from the design) does not match the price point when compared to its competitors. As with the bar girls, the 'personality' of the product had much less to do with the decision to buy than the 'looks'. Even if we want to believe differently.

Bottom line is that people do judge a book by its cover.

Take the time to make sure your products and services look the best. Make sure your website is designed by a professional, make sure sales letters are clean and well laid out, make sure digital products have sexy product images and generally make sure that anything related to your business looks professional.

# CONTROLLING YOUR MAN

*"The power of unfulfilled desires is
the root of all man's slavery"*

Paramahansa Yogananda

We have already spoken a little about desire. Here we should focus on it purely as a marketing strategy.

After a bar girl has caught the attention of a passing gentleman her next job is to create desire (if her looks and the way she has dressed have not already succeeded in doing this). After the initial desire is created it must then be built up.

To do this she will work his ego with compliments, continue to slowly expose a little more of herself and start touching the guy in ways that only a girl should. This over the course of one or two drinks is often enough to build the desire to a point that the man can no longer say no.

However, the girl needs to be careful to not go too far in her efforts to build desire.

I was invited out to a strip bar by a friend of mine who lives in Pattaya. I don't drink, but I had never been to a strip club before so in the name of research (and just to be social of course) I went along.

Seats surrounded the central stage and we sat down to watch the show. Not far from me was a tourist who had gained the interest of one of the girls (who was wearing nothing but a very small bikini). She was certainly doing a great job of building desire...

Sliding her immaculate body up against his and guiding his hand to touch her all over he was visibly uhmmm, excited. She continued to build this desire like a true professional, slowly stroking his 'excitement'.

Problem was shortly after a wet patch appeared on his trousers and he hurriedly left the club looking rather embarrassed.

Basically she has lost the sale by giving away too much in her pre-sell. It may be a graphic illustration, but you get the idea.

Your business needs to build the desire of the customer until they can no longer resist. However it also needs to be careful not to give away its services for free to a point where people no longer want to pay.

The first thing you need to do is demonstrate that you can deliver what a customer is looking for. You then need to build desire by layering the emotional benefits. Keep expanding these benefits and heightening the customers excitement.

This can be done through education, case studies, testimonials, bonuses, extra features that provide additional benefits, free trials, free samples, videos, limited time discounts etc. Just be careful not to give away too much...

Many experts suggest to over-deliver, and much of the time they are right. However, as in the case of the girl earlier, over delivering can sometimes lose a paying customer.

An example of this is often found in the online software industry. Something I know too well running such a company.

In this industry it is considered best practice to use the 'freemium' business model. This is where you give the core functionality away for free so as to build your list, and then upgrade customers to paid levels of service/functionality.

While this may work some of the time, in many tests companies have found that they actually lose paying customers, not gain them. The reason being is that many people object to paying more for something they perceive to be free, or that the free version simply meets all of their needs.

Over-delivering to the point of losing a customer is rare. But it is something to be careful of as it can and does happen.

Also rare though, is the company that will go to as much effort as the bar girls to build the desire in their prospects. There is a serious lesson here for most businesses.

# HELPING THE ENEMY

*"Competition has been shown to be useful up to a
certain point and no further; but cooperation,
which is the thing we must strive for today,
begins where competition leaves off"*

Franklin D. Roosevelt

Despite all of the competition in Pattaya the girls seem rarely to be focused on it, or worried by it. Actually they help each other.

During the evening of the 'excited customer' mentioned before, another girl was trying to seduce me. Only with very little success.

I was trying to politely ignore, despite her persistence.

(On a side note persistence is admirable and should be encouraged. But it should be done in the right way and not come across like an annoying door to door sales man. Or for that matter MLM 'business' owners – be careful before you lose your friends.)

Anyway, back to the story…

The girl was indeed persistent, and so I tried to ignore by looking at a different girl. She soon got the message, but I did not get the result I had hoped for. Instead of some peace she asked if I wanted her friend instead and began inviting her over.

I soon realised this was standard practice.

First the girls will try and get a customer for themselves. If that does not work they then see if the interests lie elsewhere. If so they will help secure the business for their competition.

This is stark contrast to much of the business world that believes in eating up your competition. Though this practice of assisting the competition is not entirely unique.

One thing silicon valley is famous for (apart for making computer chips and obscene amounts of money) is competitors helping each other.

There is one story of a business who learned of a competitors problem that would soon put them out of business. The same problem they recently had overcome themselves. Instead of keeping the information to themselves they shared it with the competitor and saved that business.

This may be quite an extreme example, but it does go to show common decency does not have to be missing when it comes to doing business.

In the internet marketing industry this cross assistance become the very fabric of the way many marketers do business. They start by building leads in a niche and trying to sell these leads a product. Regardless of whether this sale is successful or not they then promote other products in the same niche, often a direct competitor's product, to this same list.

The reason this works so well is that if the customer was going to buy from them then chances are they would already have done so. If they did not buy your product then maybe they want someone else's.

If you help them find the product they are looking for you can make a commission.

Ironically perhaps, the most commissions are usually made from someone who did already buy your product. This is because someone looking for what you are selling will often want more of the same (this will of course depend on your product or service).

For example if you sell information on real estate investing then a customer is likely to buy a lot of information on this topic, not just yours. For the bar girls they know that most customers are likely to want more than one girl during their holiday.

When customers are in a buying mode we can take advantage of this to get commissions from our competition, regardless of whether a prospect decides to buy from us or not.

Think which of your competitors you can team up with instead of which you are trying to compete against. Think co-operation, not competition.

Another danger in focusing on your competition is getting lost in trying to be the same as them.

In my own business we have several competitors, and anytime we look at them we start getting caught up in thinking we must have their features or their design.

This is not to say there is no value in 'borrowing' ideas. However it can distract you from being you. From your own creativity and uniqueness that may well result in your success.

There are only so many hours in the day. If you spend too many of these hours worrying about the competition and chasing them, then you will become an industry clone, not an industry leader.

# BEYOND SEX

*"A shoe without sex appeal is like a tree without leaves. Service without emotion is like a shoe without sex appeal"*

Anonymous

As with any business a prostitute will find repeat business easier than getting new business.

No need to find the customer, grab attention, spend time making the sale and then agreeing on a price. All the preliminary hard work has been done, yet the profit remains the same.

Basically this means they end up making more money for less effort.

If a bar girl in Pattaya wants to get repeat business she must do her job very well as competition is fierce. And let's be honest, the guys there are not looking for long term commitment.

However if the service is exceptional then why risk going anywhere else? For most customers they are there on a holiday and will have limited time. If they get a great girl they are more likely to stick with her for the duration of their stay.

I have no doubt that many a guy ended up going back to some girl and spending far more than he intended due to exceptional service.

Thankfully I doubt you will need to perform the level of service or compete at the level these girls do. But that does not mean you can be lazy either.

We all know the frustration of poor quality sales support, and then worse, poor quality customer service after a purchase.

When we contact a company and get an immediate, helpful response we are always impressed. When we go to a café and the waitress remembers our name, favourite drink and gives us a friendly smile it makes the experience of drinking coffee so much more than just a good drink.

Look to see what you can do to improve the attitude of your team and the quality of your service. Consider how you would want to be treated, and then do even better.

Look for ways to add a little extra to your customer experience to make them feel special. It does not need to be much or cost a lot, so long as it is effective.

For example a few years ago I went for a massage in the local shop to me. It was the first time I had been there but I was greeted with a smile and treated like an old friend.

Even though I was only getting a Thai massage the girl first washed my feet in warm water and fresh limes. She bought me water and escorted me to the massage room.

The massage itself was good, and afterwards I felt nicely relaxed. When I got changed and went to pay I was sat down to a cup of herbal tea, more water and fresh fruit. The girls were friendly and chatted with no mention of the money and no urgency to go anywhere.

This was the perfect end to a great massage. And this attitude and additional service paid off. I continued to go to the same shop every week for the next 3 years. My regular girl left and opened her own shop so I now go there.

The massage itself is good, though I know I can find better. However the experience is much more than just the massage. It is this type of experience you want to look at delivering to your customers.

If you are in the information business look at ways to continue to deliver additional material, organize expert interviews or provide free unadvertised resources.

If you run a local store greet customers with a smile, ask them how they are, have occasional free treats for them (perhaps a chocolate or a candy for their children) or maybe give them a random discount or free gift just for being a customer.

If you have a regular service such as window cleaning or dry cleaning give your customers a scratch card and a discount voucher on their birthday or at Christmas.

There are many ways to let customers know you care and to make them feel special. We all like to feel appreciated, and when customers feel this they will not only come back for more, but tell others too.

# NOT ALL MEN WERE CREATED EQUAL

*"You are serving a customer, not a life sentence.*
*Learn how to enjoy your work"*

Laurie McIntosh

I live mostly in Chiang Mai (northern Thailand) where there are many Westerners living with Thai wives or girlfriends. They are usually just typical relationships. Pattaya is very different.

Don't get me wrong, my friend who lives there has a wife and children, so normal relationships do exist. However most of the Thai-Western couples you see there are working girls with their customers.

As I was walking around the streets it struck me that of all these 'business' relationships there were two distinct types. Those girls who looked like it was painful hard work, and those that looked like they were genuinely enjoying themselves.

Not surprising those who looked miserable were escorting unattractive, overweight miserable looking old men. Those having fun were with someone much closer to their own age, matched in appearance and were being treated more like a girlfriend than a prostitute (ie with some respect).

While not all relationships are quite that black and white, it did make me realize the importance of choosing the right customer.

Some girls were focused on taking any business they could find, others seemed more selective. And while their looks did appear to play a part in this ability to select the quality of their customer, it was not as much as you would think.

It does go to show another advantage to providing a higher quality service though – you are able to be more selective about your cliental.

All of these girls were doing the same job. Yet some had learned to have fun at the same time and to make the best of their situation. Others put money ahead of enjoyment.

It is my belief that every business owner should enjoy the business they choose. However, 'bad' customers can make this challenging at times.

I have heard it said before that you should 'fire' your bad customers, maintain your average customers and focus your attention on the top 20%. However while walking around Pattaya I was struck by the graphic importance of this.

Even in the software business I encourage my customer support team to suggest a refund to dissatisfied or problem customers. Of course we try to help them, but if they are just going to cause a headache for my team I would rather let them go.

(Just to clarify – we don't fire customers just because they have a problem. Actually a lot of satisfaction is gained by helping resolve a customer's issues. It's only if they have a negative attitude and cause the customer support team to become unhappy.)

If you want business to be fun then look at how you can improve the quality of your customers.

One internet marketer once told me how he ran two membership sites. One at $47/month, the other at $247/month. He said that the customers in the cheaper program always expected more for less and caused the most amount of support requests.

Those in the higher priced program were much better quality customers. They caused less headache, and generated more profit.

He is not alone. My own experience as a therapist saw the same phenomena.

When I first started treating clients my confidence (and experience) was low. I charged a low price accordingly. The customers I attracted were hard work. Most just wanted someone to blame, and they were always looking to save money where they could.

After I worked on many of my limiting beliefs I decided to increase my price – dramatically. I became one of the highest priced therapists in Auckland virtually overnight.

Also virtually overnight my client base changed.

Gone were the whiners, whingers and blamers. Instead I started seeing clients that were serious about change. They valued their time and mine. They always paid on time and never complained about the price.

Look to your own business to see how you can increase the quality of your customers.

Pass on those you don't want to a competitor. There is always someone willing to pay you for your rubbish.

Ensure you are advertising in the right places and charging the right amount. If you have resistance to this then check your beliefs. Just as I did, I suggest you dispose of your restrictive beliefs so you can dispose of your restrictive customers.

Business will take up a large part of your life, so make sure it is fun.

# 2 GIRLS ARE BETTER THAN 1

*"You are never strong enough that you don't need help"*

César Chávez

Most of the girls who arrive in Pattaya have never worked in the sex industry before. Many have had little experience of westerners or western culture. And if you want to see the worst elements of western culture, then head to Pattaya.

For these girls to survive they need to learn fast. And the best way to learn is to find a mentor.

There is so much to learn – Where to find work, how to snare a customer, how to set a price, where they can go to provide services, what type of services are expected and the language used to describe them, how to handle drunk customers and the police...

I was really impressed by the way the girls look after each other. While this is very much a part of Thai culture (caring and looking after each other) it is also essential for both their success and their survival.

In the world of the entrepreneur there is a tendency to try and be independent, or to think that someone 'higher up' would not have the time to help someone starting out. Neither are good attitudes to have.

I am both independent and stubborn. These character traits can be a blessing and a burden. I have had to learn I can't do everything myself, and sometimes help or guidance from someone more experienced can save me a lot of time and frustration.

I don't know anyone who has 'made it' who did not get the support and guidance from someone more experienced than them. Whether formal mentoring or informal guidance help from others is critical – we just need to learn to ask for, and accept it.

The other misconception is that those who are more successful won't have time for you. While this may be true some of the time, it is also untrue much of the time.

People who become successful in any industry are almost certainly passionate to the extreme about what it is they do. And like a nerd in any niche you try and shut them up about their pet passion.

Forget a dinner party, they will bore an entire stadium of people who don't care if given half a chance.

And yes – I include myself in this group. I have been told to shut up about business and marketing on more than one inappropriate occasion.

So when I find someone who will not only listen, but is actually interested too, it is like a kid finding a candy store.

Having had many people help me over the years, and having assisted many others I can say the one thing a mentor loves more than anything else is to see someone taking action.

There is nothing more frustrating than to spend hours giving advice only to see it ignored completely.

And here lies the key to securing the help from those who have gone before you. Demonstrate action. If you can learn to listen and then prove that you are a doer and not a talker, you will find many people willing to give you their time.

And just as a bar girls friends can help her find a place to work, assist her with getting and managing her first customers and knowing which are the best hotels to use, so too can your mentors provide essential contacts and networks.

My hope is that you will not only seek out, ask for and make use of mentors, but that one day you too will then help others to succeed. This mentor-student relationship is perhaps one of the most rewarding in business.

# THE HONEST CRIMINAL

*"Honesty is the best policy
- when there is money in it"*

Mark Twain

I forget who said it, but one famous person once said prostitution is the only honest form of business.

While it may be an extreme and technically not true statement, there is something to be said for it.

Once again, judgement aside, usually with prostitution the deal is clear and open. There is a straight forward transaction where both the girl and her customer know and understand the business agreement.

But this is not always the case...

I have a friend who shall remain nameless. He recently arrived in Thailand and decided to experiment with the local girls. Only problem is he did not understand the rules of the game he was playing.

You see in Thailand some bar girls will not say a price unless asked. They don't want to appear as a prostitute, and giving a price would essentially make them one. That said they still expect a 'gift' in the morning.

And this is where the problem began. My friend was unaware of this expectation. He thought he was playing by home rules, and that the girl just wanted him for his good looks.

When she started hinting that he may want to 'help' her with a little money for her mother he become annoyed. The transaction had not been spelled out to him, and he was unaware of the fine print.

He is hardly alone in this situation. It is a common story for those living in Thailand. However this grey area of the sex industry is far from alone in the lack of clarity and regular misunderstanding.

Some businesses simply expect customers to understand what is, or what is not, included in a price or service. Others are out right deceitful.

Either way the customer is the one who walks away annoyed and is unlikely to return. They are also highly likely to bad mouth the business to anyone who will listen.

Your job is to ensure that prospects know exactly what to expect before you allow them to become a customer.

Be honest about what is or what is not included, and about any additional charges they may incur at a later date. Most people are fine with this so long as they know in advance.

It is when people find out after that they feel they have been cheated. And no ones like to feel they have been taken advantage of.

# F..K YOU

*"I don't see how you can write anything
of value if you don't offend someone"*

Marvin Harris

Perhaps what makes Pattaya so successful is its openness about what it is. Nothing is hidden around this controversial industry.

Controversy has always created curiosity. Here people feel free to explore this curiosity whether it is purely as an observer like myself (and there are plenty of observers of all ages, genders and nationalities) or as a participant looking to experience something different.

One thing is for sure, Pattaya generates a lot of money by being openly controversial.

Now while it may be true this book was inspired by Pattaya, as a marketer I have exploited this angle of controversy to help market the book.

I could have just written a normal book about business and marketing principles. But by putting them into a controversial context it makes these dry principles far more interesting, intriguing and most importantly marketable.

In my blog (www.FusionDojo.com) I often take a controversial position on many normal business and marketing teachings. However I don't just make something controversial for the sake of being controversial.

You will often see many lower quality celebrities or writers do this. They will do or say something just to get attention. There is little purpose or thought in their point of controversy. Just attention grabbing.

Instead look to find why your opinion is different, or how you can use a more taboo topic to get attention and to illustrate your message.

Controversy can work in several ways.

Firstly it can help get you free exposure. The media loves controversy. You can pay thousands for advertising, or get it for free by having the right newsworthy angle.

Secondly it grabs more attention (which is why the media love it). Not only does it get more attention, it is also more memorable. Things that are the 'same same' blend into the background. If something stands out like proverbial dogs balls, people will take notice and remember.

Thirdly controversy gets people emotional. It creates debate and gets people talking. This can help spread your message via word of mouth.

Controversy is more an art than an exact science.

You don't want to alienate potential customers, or create so much offense that papers won't even print anything about you. However you do need to create enough to get attention and have impact.

At the same time make sure to keep it relevant and intelligent. This will make your efforts far more effective.

# WHO IS IN CONTROL?

*"Conceit is bragging about yourself. Confidence means you believe you can get the job done"*

Johnny Unitas

When your competition outnumbers your potential customer base at least 2 or 3 to 1 you need to have confidence. Especially if many of your prospects are too shy to approach you.

For the girls in Pattaya this is a daily (or nightly) problem.

They must learn to have confidence in themselves, to literally sell themselves. And for a culture that by its nature is more quiet and reserved this is quite a feat.

If you walk around Pattaya you will see some girls who are either naturally more confident and extrovert, or who have learned to overcome this shyness out of necessity, talking to and interacting with prospects and customers.

Those who lack this confidence sit in the background hoping for someone to approach them. Do they make money? Probably. But certainly not as much as those who are confident and proactive.

So where does confidence come from?

Unfortunately for many of the girls in Pattaya drugs and alcohol contribute a lot. Hopefully you can tap in to other sources. The truth is though few of us are confident until we have done something often enough.

Remember the first time you learned to ride a bike or drive a car. At first you had zero skill and probably very little confidence. With practice your skills grew and so did your confidence until you no longer even thought about it.

Where confidence is concerned there is a certain amount of truth to the old adage 'fake it until you make it'.

Several years back I suffered from a spontaneous pneumothorax, basically a collapsed lung for no apparent reason. (Apparently not all that uncommon for tall Caucasian males in there early twenties. Who knew.)

While in hospital this young doctor was telling me the two possible procedures in my situation. One was to cut through the muscle in the side of the ribs, the other to plunge a needle through the front of the chest to just the right depth.

The second operation he told me he had never seen carried out before, though the first option was more common it was extremely painful for a long time after.

Shortly after telling me this, the senior doctor announced they would be going with the huge needle through the chest choice – and the young doctor (who had never seen this operation) would be performing it.

I still remember his face as he pushed the needle in. He looked more worried than I did. Not exactly a good way to instil confidence.

And here is the thing... if you don't act confident you will struggle to build trust with a prospect, customer or client. They need to believe in you.

Confidence alone is enough to get money from someone as shown time and again by con men (and women). Con being short for confidence trickster.

Not exactly the most ethical way to do business, but you get the point. Having confidence in your business is critical to its success.

Use techniques such as hypnosis, NLP or EFT to help you remove any hesitations or superficial fears if you need to. And don't be afraid to fake it until you make it real if you have to (so long as nobody is at risk).

Remember real confidence comes from a belief in yourself, and this belief can be contagious. Believe in yourself enough and others will believe in you too

# BUYING BOOBS

*"Understanding how to be a good investor
makes you a better business manager"*

Charlie Munger

Few places in this world are girls competing with breast size as much as in Pattaya. And while there are plenty of guys who like them small it does not stop girls wishing they had more.

For many an increase in breast size will literally result in an increase in income.

They know this all too well. And so with the help of some savings, or a kind 'sponsor', more and more girls are opting for implants.

It is easy to be cynical or criticize such actions, but we are not in their position. The sad truth is that after surgery many girls will be able to make more money.

The cost of the surgery in Thailand is between $1000 and $2000. A working girl can typically make between $1000 and $3000 in a month (can be more for the high class ones). This means that a 30% increase in customers, and an increase in their nightly fee, could pay off the investment in just 1-4 months.

This is an investment that will keep paying long after the initial costs have been covered. If only all business investments were that certain and that long lasting.

For the rest of us investing in our business is usually a much more careful balance. We need to ensure we spend enough to provide a quality product or service, while not overspending and putting the business (or ourselves) at financial risk.

An example from early in my own business was the decision to hire an office manager.

Technically I could do the work myself, so as a start-up entrepreneur my immediate response was that it would be a waste of money. However the problem was that the marketing for the company was suffering as that was my real skill.

By hiring the manager I freed up a lot more of my time, and was soon able to increase the company revenue as a direct result of that free time. This more than covered the cost of the manager.

She was a big investment.

I won't embarrass myself with some of my mistakes (and there have been plenty). The reality is that unless you are a living miracle you won't get it right every time.

However that does not mean should not at least try.

Think it through carefully. Is holding on to the cash just being tight? Or is spending it just frivolous or feeding the ego. (There have been many a company gone broke because of 'investing' in a fancy office or unnecessary luxury car.)

The important thing though is that you do invest.

I see the lack of investment kill many business here in Thailand. They think that they only need money to open their shop/café/condo.

Once the business is open they then suck the profits out, never reinvesting back into it. This can lead to all sorts of problems such as low quality staff, lack of stock and buildings or equipment falling apart. Once the damage is done there is no money left to fix the problem.

Ensure to keep investing and reinvesting so your business can not only survive, but thrive.

# DON'T BE TOO MATURE

*"Life can only be understood backwards;
but it must be lived forwards."*

Søren Kierkegaard

Let's be honest, one of the biggest assets a prostitute has is her youth. Once this is gone so is much of her business. And the smart girls not only know this, they plan for it.

I doubt any of them really think they will be continuing in the profession for ever. In fact most only plan to be there for 1 or 2 years to make some good money and then get out.

Problem is it rarely works that way.

It is easy to get used to earning and spending more money. Unfortunately it is much harder to go from making $2000/month to $200/month (which is often the reality facing a retiring bar girl).

Therefore the smart girls save and invest their money for the future, and many are actually looking for a husband. Not exactly a strategy most westerners would consider, but for many it does work.

I know many cases of guys who are living in Thailand who are in a long term relationship with, or married to, a working girl they met in a bar.

As soon as they can find someone long term they can get out of the business. So being a prostitute can be a short term strategy to a long term solution.

Consider your own business. Is it built for the long term? Can it survive technological or social change? Or is it even what you want to do for the long term?

For many people the answer is no.

Look at companies that built fax machines, or cell phone companies that were slow to adopt to the increasing demand in smart phones. There are many examples throughout history of business models that failed due to their inability to adapt or change.

Then there are the countless business owners that build businesses and get stuck in them long after they want to leave. They become addicted to the cash flow, but have built no exit strategy.

Be sure to engineer your business to be flexible in its growth, and systematized to run without you. Once your business can run with or without you, then you have an asset you can sell. This is a very respectable exit strategy.

Life is full of unforeseen events. As I type this I am sat here unable to walk for a few weeks due to a recent motorbike accident.

Thankfully my business runs in a way that it does not need me. Had I been a bar girl (thankfully not much of an option for me!) then my income would have disappeared.

Truth is I was in this dangerous situation before when I worked as a therapist. Luckily I had no problems at that time, but it is a risk that many small business owners live with every day.

You need to plan for both the expected and the unexpected. Make sure you have systems in place and start with the end in mind

# PROSTITUTES THAT SUCK

*"Our attitude towards others determines
their attitude towards us"*

Earl Nightingale

Attitude is critical in any business. And walking around Pattaya you can see plenty of attitude. Problem is most of it is the wrong type.

If you are trying to attract a client then a friendly, welcoming and approachable attitude would be an obvious choice. Yet many of the girls appear to have become bitter, angry and aggressive. Perhaps in part fuelled by too much alcohol.

Once again, this is not to say they don't get any customers. They do. However if we are looking at running an optimal business then we are looking to get the maximum number of customers as possible.

Those who smile, are genuinely friendly and are caring certainly do much better.

This is hardly a major revelation. Yet as mentioned before, any business should be aware of the impact that its staff's attitude have on each other, and on the customer.

In my opinion if all businesses were to place proper importance on attitude when hiring, most people would be without a job.

Think of all the times when you were greeted by a shop assistant, waitress, sales personnel or customer support who had a bad attitude. Or the number of places you have worked where some of the other staff bitched about each other or performed their tasks with a less than enthusiastic attitude.

Sure not everyone will be high spirited every day or get on 100% with everyone else. But some people appear to be just born with a chip on their shoulder and are simply best avoided.

Skills can be taught. A new attitude is much harder to cultivate. Within my businesses I look for attitude first, skills second. Of course skills are important, but are of no use without the correct attitude.

For a prostitute it is not just her attitude with the customers, but her attitude towards herself and her choice of work. If she can't respect herself, and have a positive attitude towards her decision to be in the sex industry, then chances are she will become depressed very quickly.

This depression can not only lead to drug and alcohol dependency, but also to a reduction in the number of clients. (Who wants to sleep with a depressed girl?)

Less obvious, but just as important, is your same self-respect and positive attitude towards the business you are in. And the self-respect and positive attitude of your other team members.

As a therapist I saw job dissatisfaction and low or no self-respect and two of the biggest causes of depression and of drug abuse.

You won't find this topic raised in many business books, but I believe it is needs to be addressed for the optimal success of a business.

Cultivate a positive attitude in yourself and your team and you will not only enjoy what you do more, but your business profits will benefit too.

# SHE DID WHAT?

*"To effectively communicate, we must realize that we are all different in the way we perceive the world and use this understanding as a guide to our communication with others"*

Tony Robbins

It is not just important to understand and use the language of your customer. You need to understand their culture too.

Pattaya is a city where cultures collide and blend with two simple objectives. Make money and have sex.

The challenge for the Thai girls fresh in town is that their potential customer base has a very different culture. And usually no understanding of theirs. This requires a rapid learning curve if they are going to make it in the big city.

Actually, it means completely reprogramming themselves.

Traditional Thai culture is very conservative in regards to displays of public affection. Kissing and even holding hands in public are still seen as disrespectful. (Though this is changing in the larger cities such as Bangkok and Chiang Mai.)

Most of these girls however come from rural towns and villages. They have had little, if any, contact with westerners before and struggle to understand not only our verbal communication but also our body language. Even the food we eat takes some getting used to.

Simple things like touching someone on the top of the head or pointing your feat towards someone are considered very rude in Thai culture. Most tourists are unaware of this, so it is easy for them to cause offense. Unless that is the girls learn to adapt.

This ability to understand the cultural difference of its customers was one of the critical factors to the success of 7-11 in Asia.

7-11, for those who don't have it, is a corner store chain. Basically it's a mini supermarket supplying the daily essentials and a lot of snacks.

What they soon realized is that the snacks and essentials that Americans wanted were not the same as Asians. Even in Asia different countries had different requirements. So they adapted.

Unlike many other franchises that were rigid in delivering the same product range from store to store, 7-11 became like a chameleon. Wherever it went it kept it original shape (that of a convenience store), but adjusted its colours (stock) to suit its new environment.

McDonalds too took a similar though not quite as an extreme approach. Unlike 7-11 whose customers were mostly locals, McDonald's customer base included many Americans travelling abroad, and who wanted American food.

They kept their core product line, but then added a couple of local variations to appeal more to the local tastes.

Many other successful franchises who have not learned to adapt in this way have either struggled or failed completely. Make sure you understand your customers.

But it is not just customers. Team members and outsourcers need to be understood too if you are to run a successful business.

I have now worked on projects with people from at least 17 different countries. Each time there is some cultural understanding needed to avoid offending the team members, to avoid a lot of frustration and to get the most out of them.

All too often I have seen the ignorance or arrogance of a project owner lead to failure. They expect everyone to understand the way they do business, but don't take the time to understand how others work.

Indian culture for example can be very frustrating to me. They have the need to please the boss and agree to do what is required, even if it is impossible. So if you ask 'when can this task be finished?' they will ask 'when does it need to be done?' Then often agree to do it in that time frame.

It's not that they mean to lie to you, it is just part of the culture to have to agree to the bosses requests.

Thai and Filipino staff have the annoying habit of not saying when they don't understand, or if there is a problem. To them this shows they are not good enough, and so are afraid to say anything to the 'boss'.

We have learned to recognize and adapt to these traits now, and it has paid off.

Look at both interactions with your customers and with your team members and see where some cultural understanding may pay off for you.

# PIMPING

*"All fighters are prostitutes and all promoters are pimps"*

Larry Holmes

The final lesson is one of scalability.

A girl can only see so many customers in one day. Most prefer only 2-4 in one week. This limits the amount of money they make.

If they want to make more money, they must see more clients, or increase their price. And there is a practical limit to both of these. In addition to this there is also a limit to their working life as age catches up on them.

So what is the solution?

Be a pimp of course.

If you can find customers and connect them to other girls, and take a commission of course, then you are only limited by the number of customers and staff you can find. And best of all you don't need to do the hard work yourself.

In Thailand it is 'Mama San' who looks after her girls. It is also her that gets the wealthiest.

I have seen all too often business owners and internet marketers chasing the short term cash. They are like a prostitute living from client to client. If they stopped working they would soon be in trouble.

I am sure you have heard the expressions 'Work on your business, not in your business' or 'Make your business work for you, not you work for your business'. Well this is usually not possible when you first start, but it is something you should have a clear plan to achieve.

Not only because it allows you to free up your time more, but it forces you to create systems, structures and a team than enable you to scale your business too.

You may find yourself in a catch 22 where you need more money and can't afford 'another girl' to do the work for you, or to 'rent a club of your own'. However also know that you are the only one who can break this catch 22.

Don't wait for 'one day'. One day never comes until you decide it does. Dramatic results often require dramatic actions.

You can't go from a single working girl to owning a large chain of bars and have hundreds of girls working for you over night. You can however start taking actions steps today to achieve that.

If you have been in business a while and you continue to operate the way you have been, then you will likely continue to see the same results.

If your plans are for more and you are tired of being the prostitute, then today is the day to become the pimp.

# CLIMAX

*"The best minds are not in government.
If any were, business would steal them away"*

Ronald Reagan

Business is business.

It does not matter if you are a prostitute or a lawyer, a shop owner or an internet entrepreneur. While each may have its own unique ways to do things the basic principles that underlie business and marketing remain the same.

The great thing about the unique environment of Pattaya is that it graphically illustrates these principles, and shows that you don't need to be a Harvard graduate to make use of them.

Your challenge is to ensure that you don't only understand, but also implement each of these concepts in your business.

Hopefully this book has inspired you to take action (working on your business – not going to Pattaya!). If so then there is little else to be said. You will be eager to put down this book and get started now…

"Nothing is really work unless you
would rather be doing something else"

J.M. Barrie

*Climax*